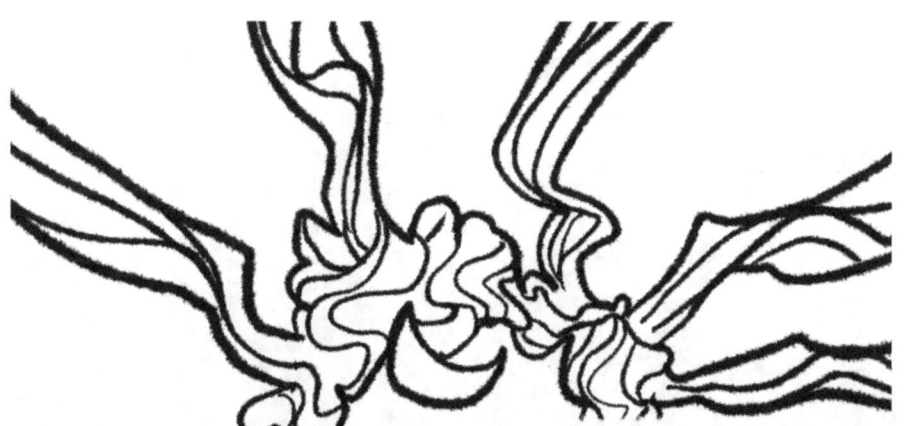

THIS BOOK BELONGS TO

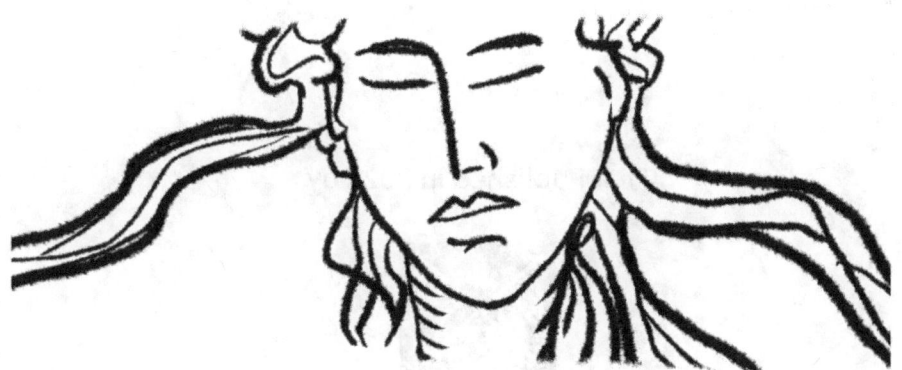

ALSO BY SEAN WOODWARD
Dia De Los Muertos
COLOURIX
Atlantean Witchcraft
ARCHONIX: The Chronicles of Leng
Typhonian Rites of Amenta
Erzulie of the Deep
Keys to the Hoodoo Kingdom
The Grimoire of ZAL
The Carrefour Tarot
Tarot of the Emissary
Gholem Tharot

VISIT SEANWODWARD.COM for latest news

First Published in 2021 by

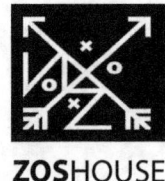

ZOSHOUSE

ISBN: 9798713056230
© 2021 Sean Woodward

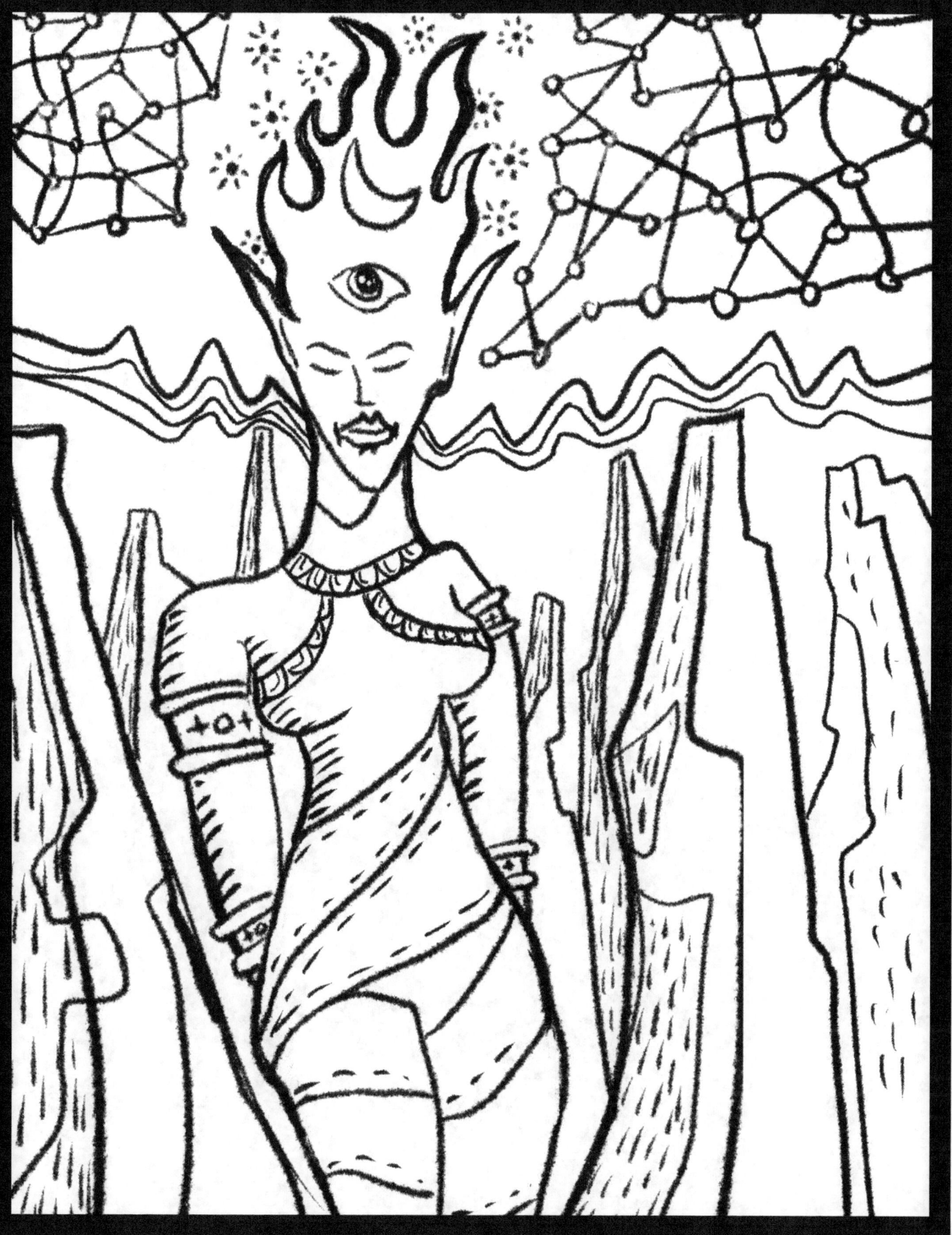

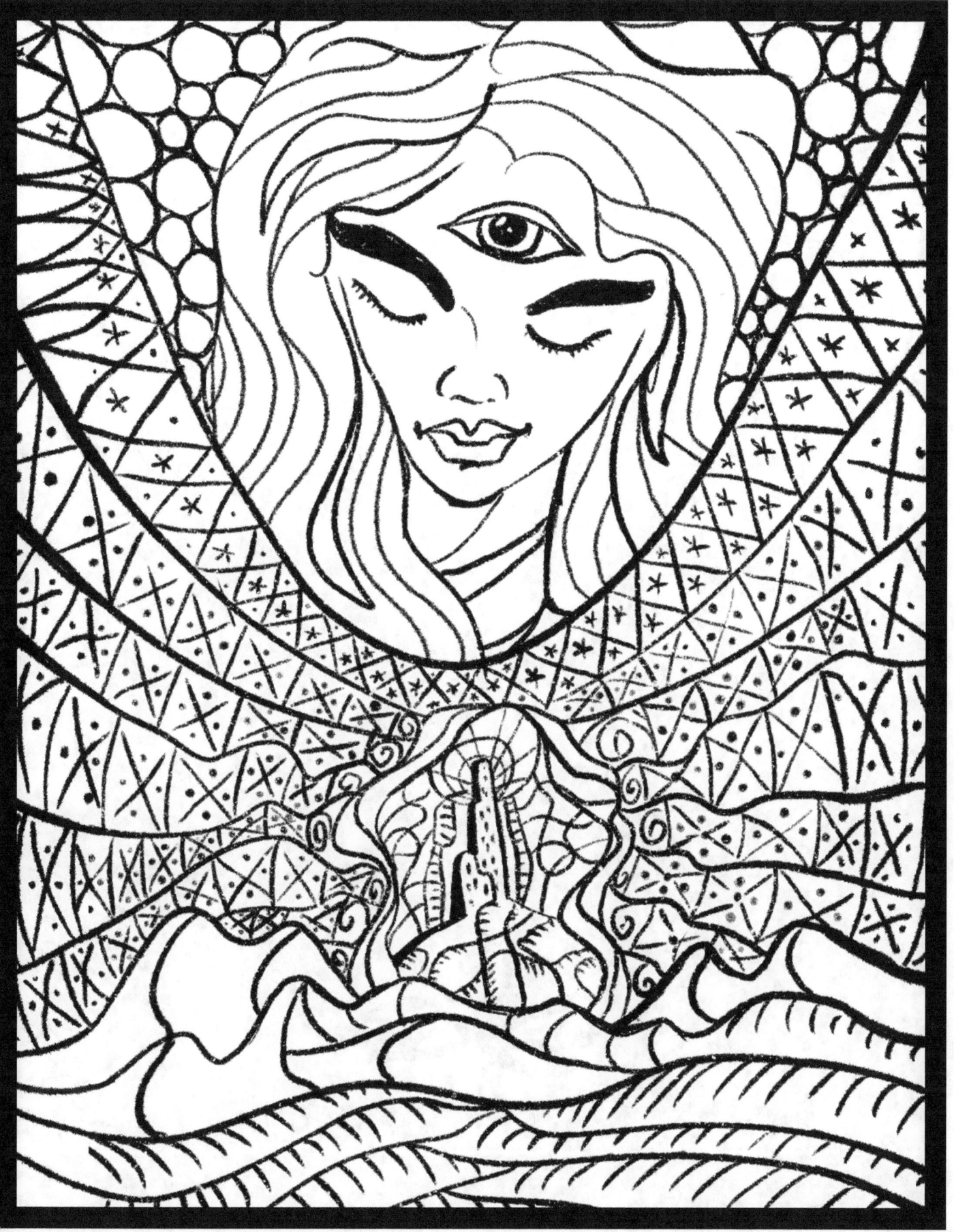

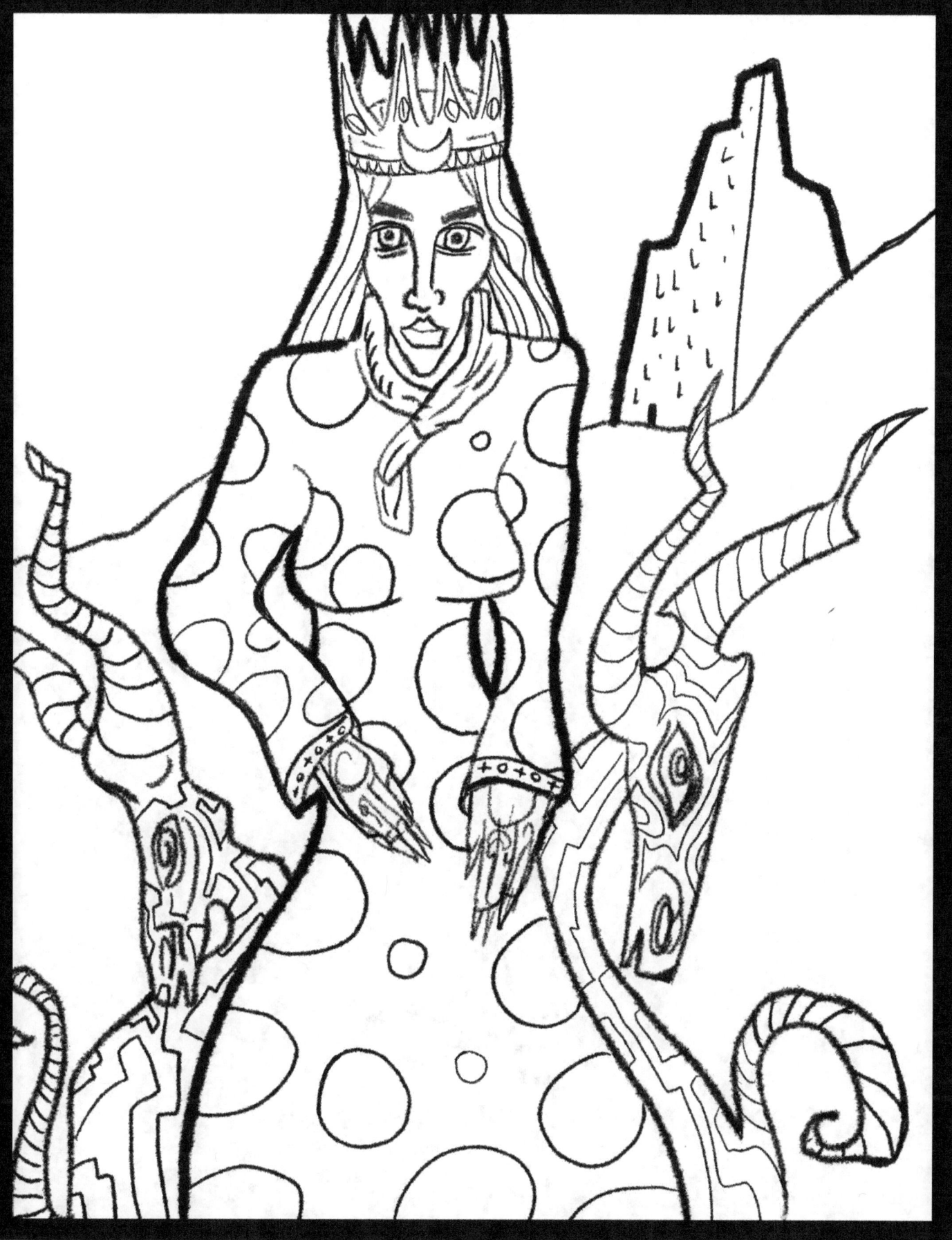

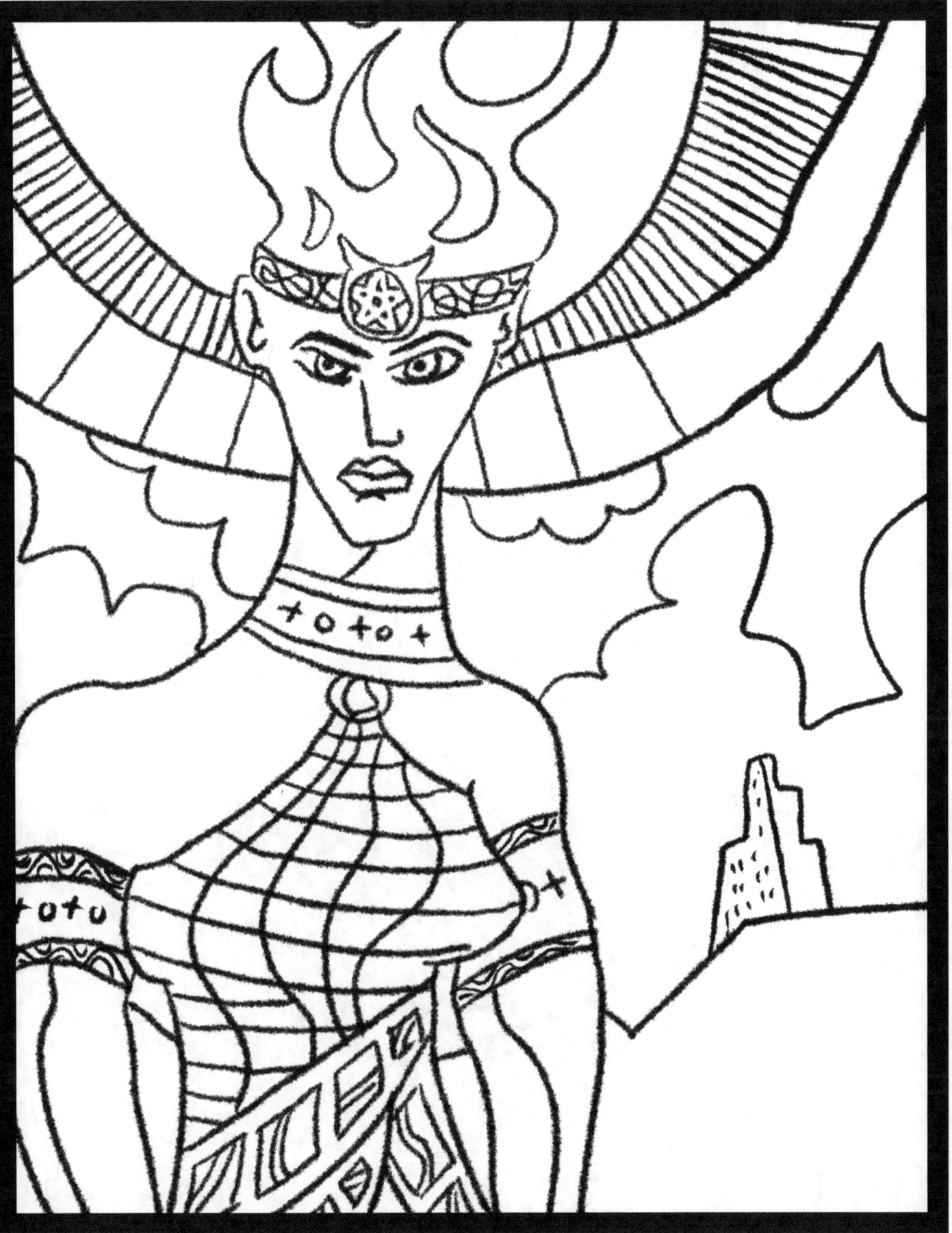

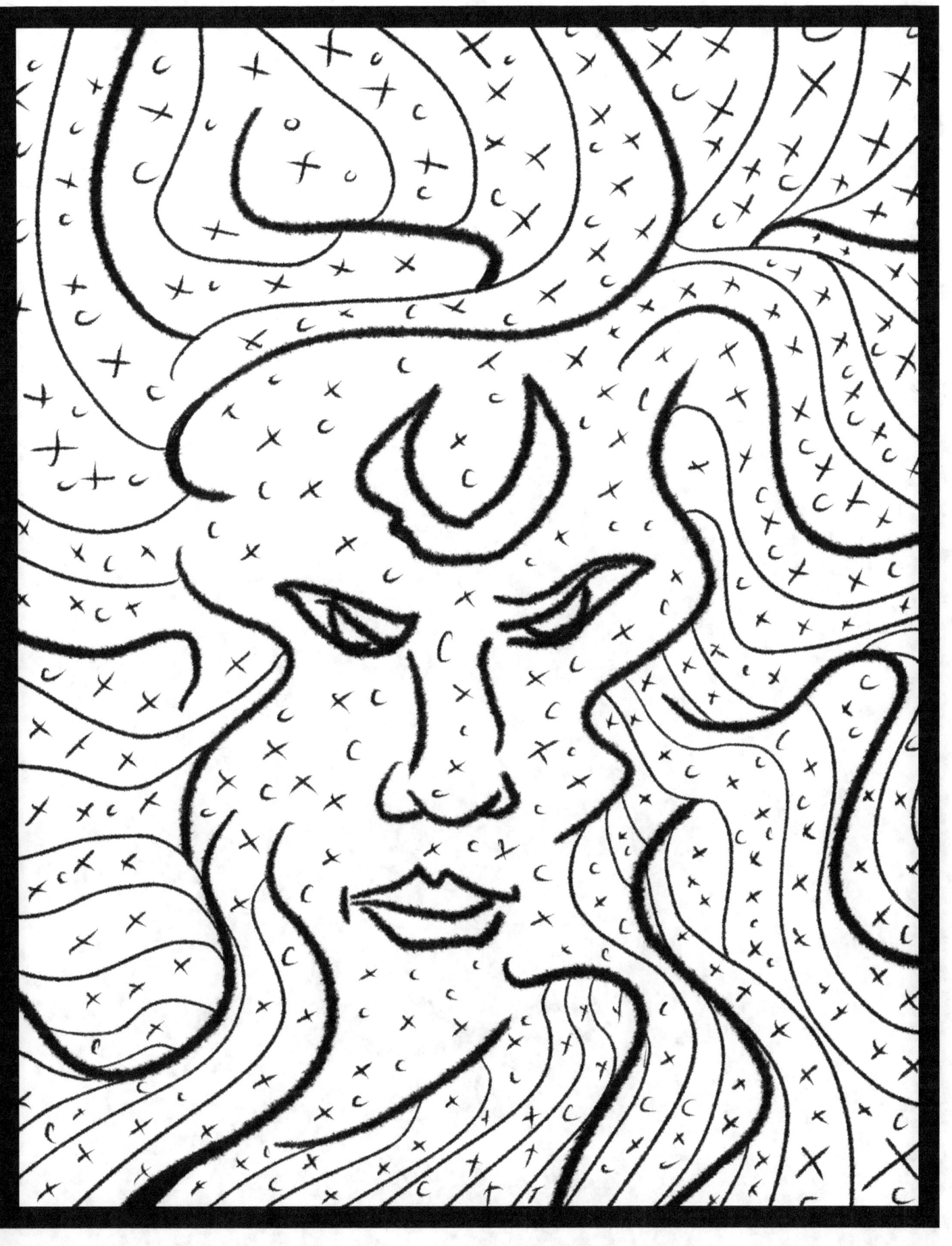

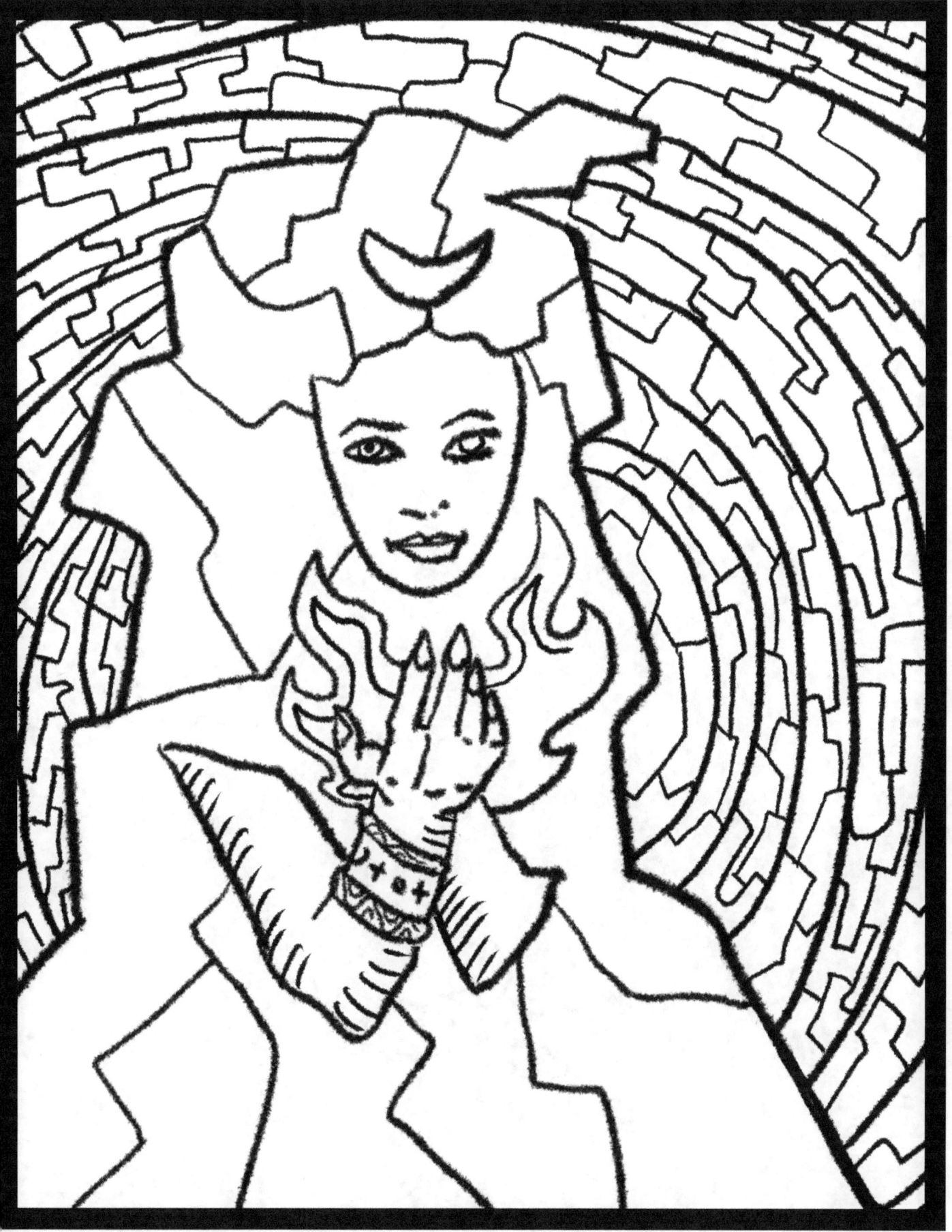

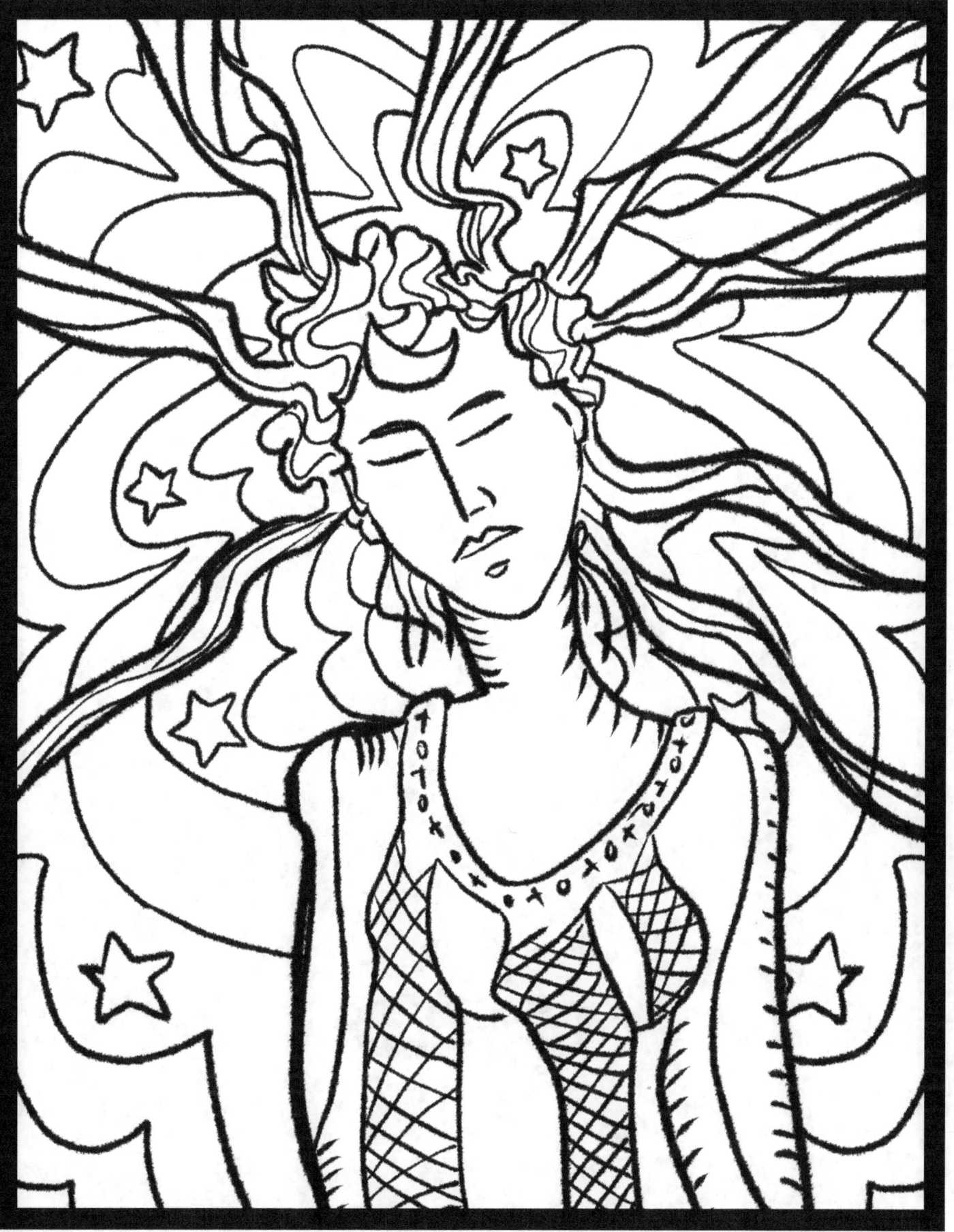

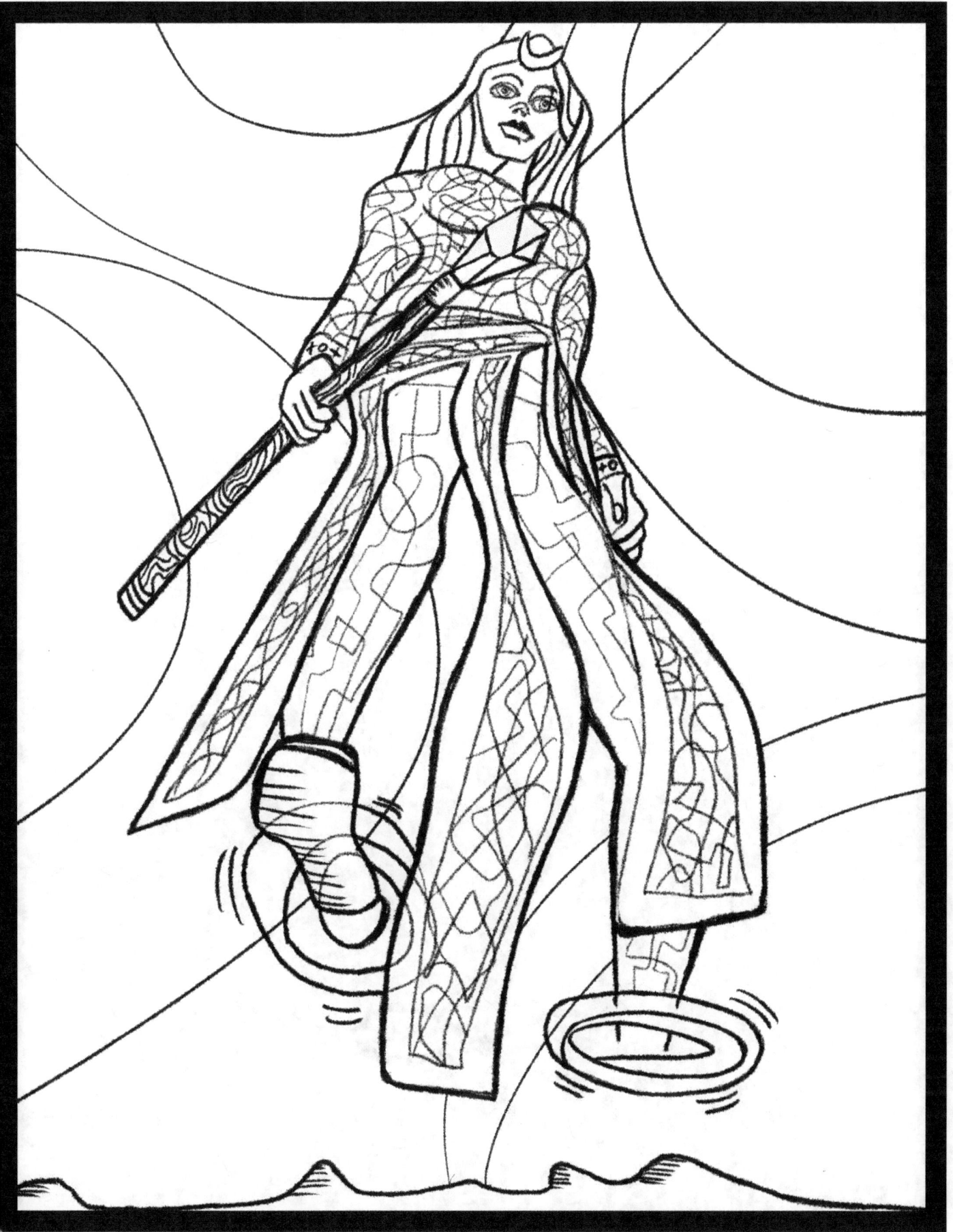

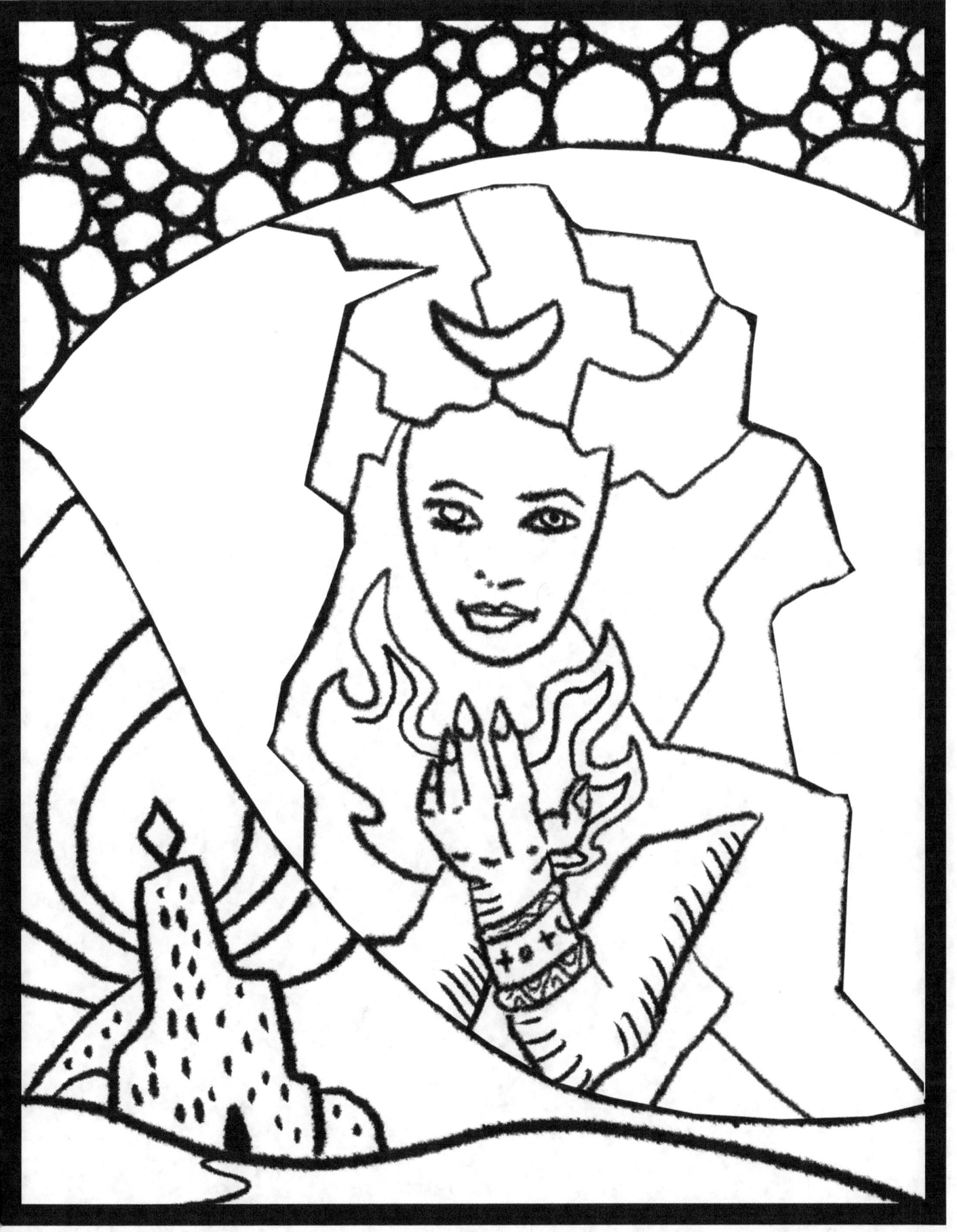

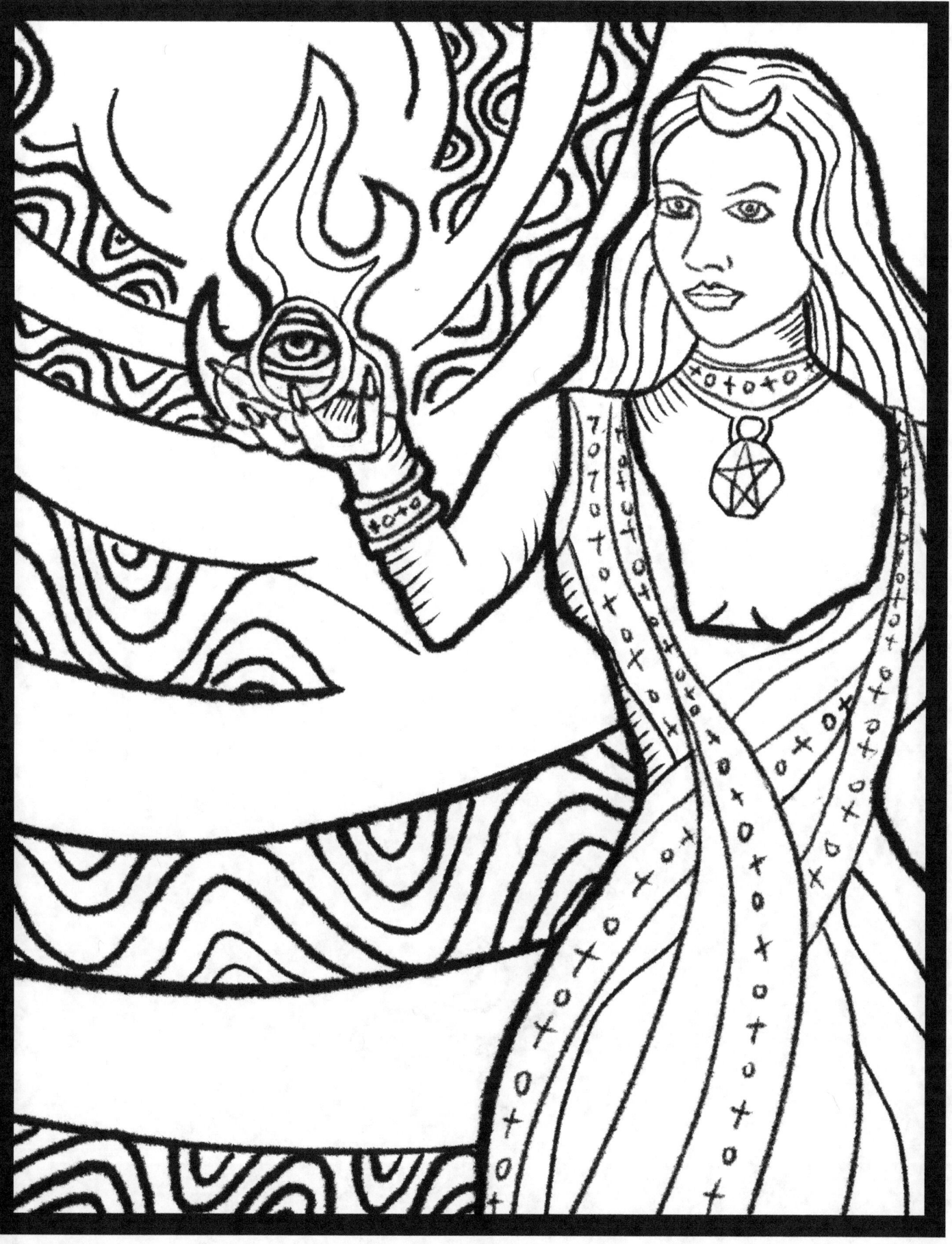

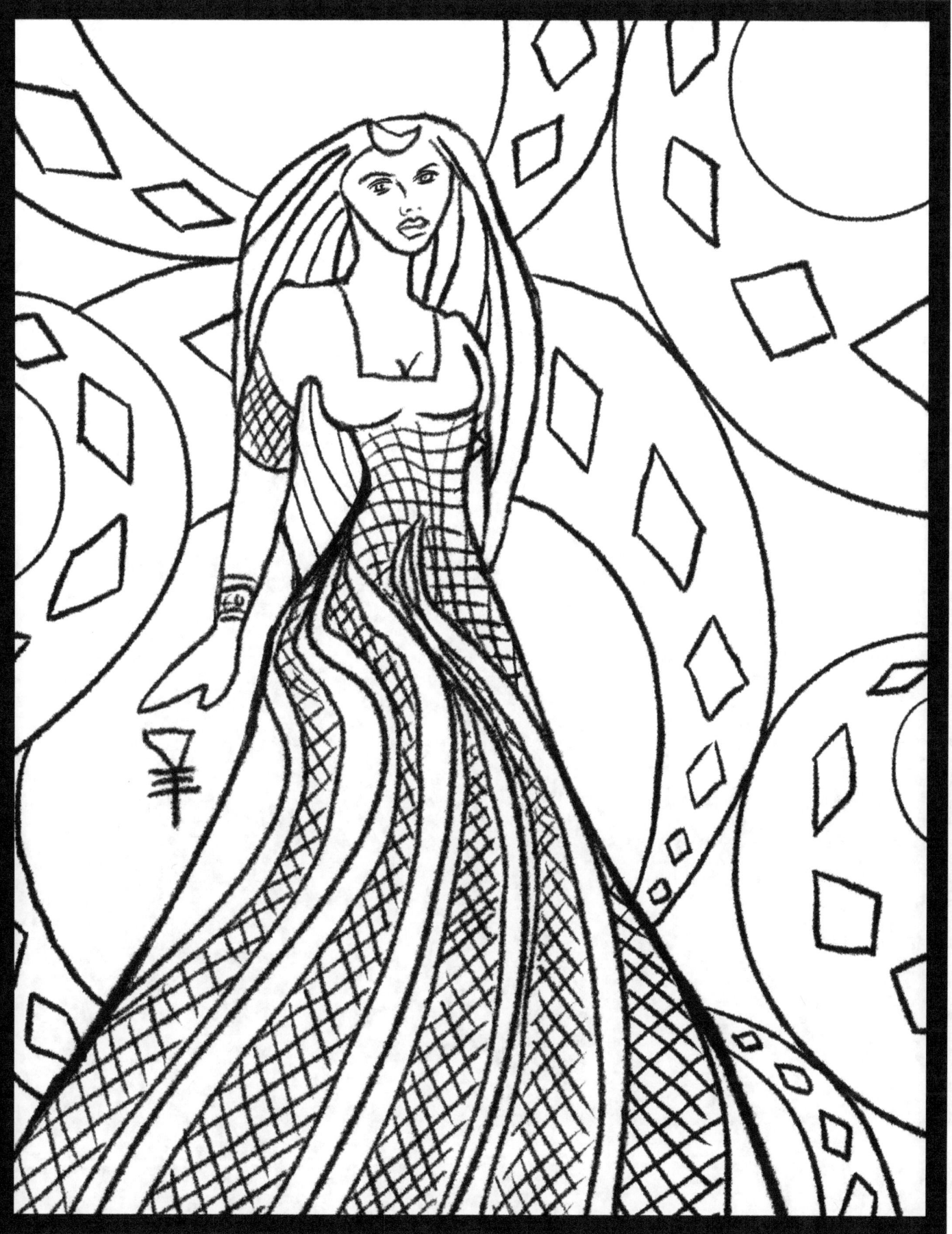

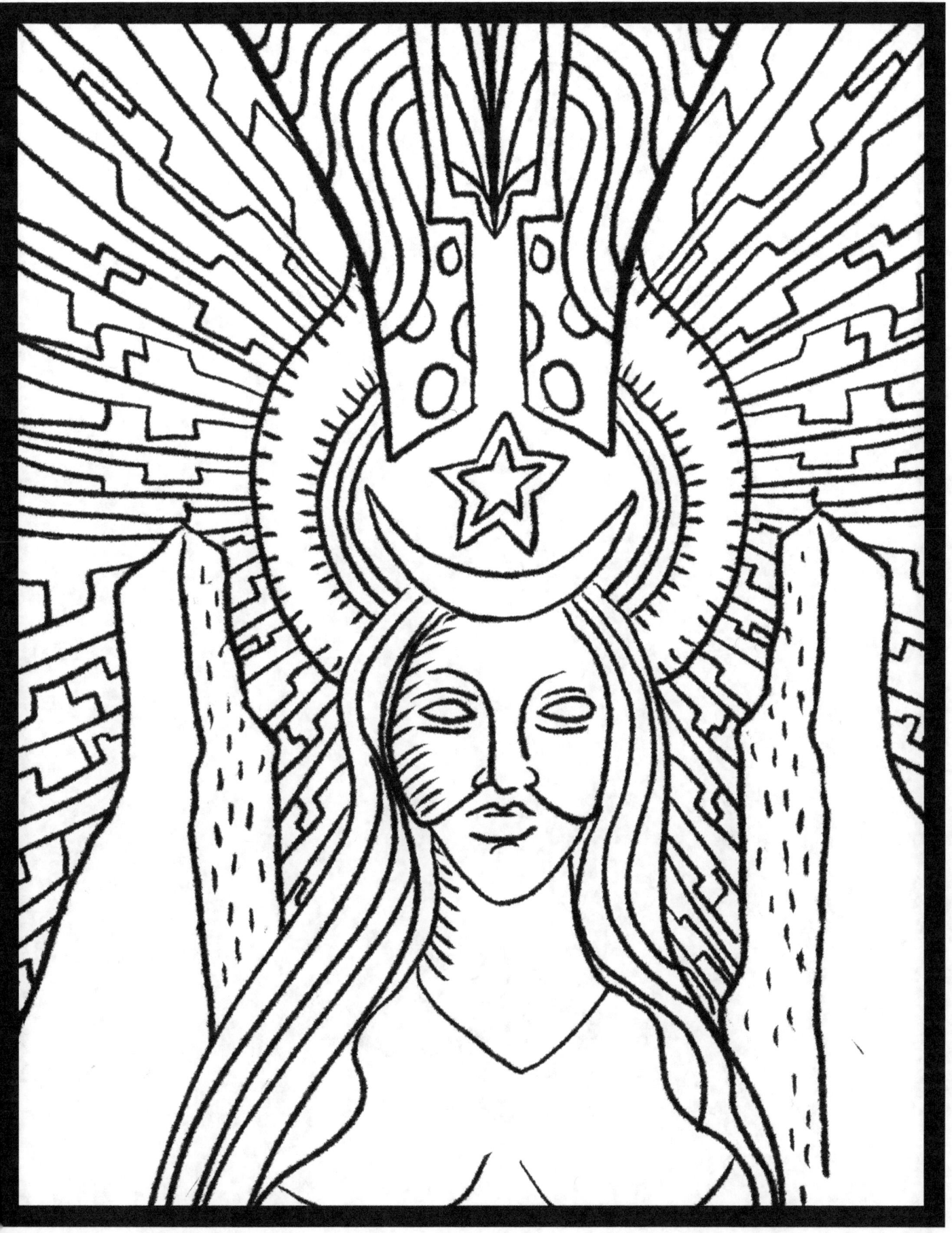

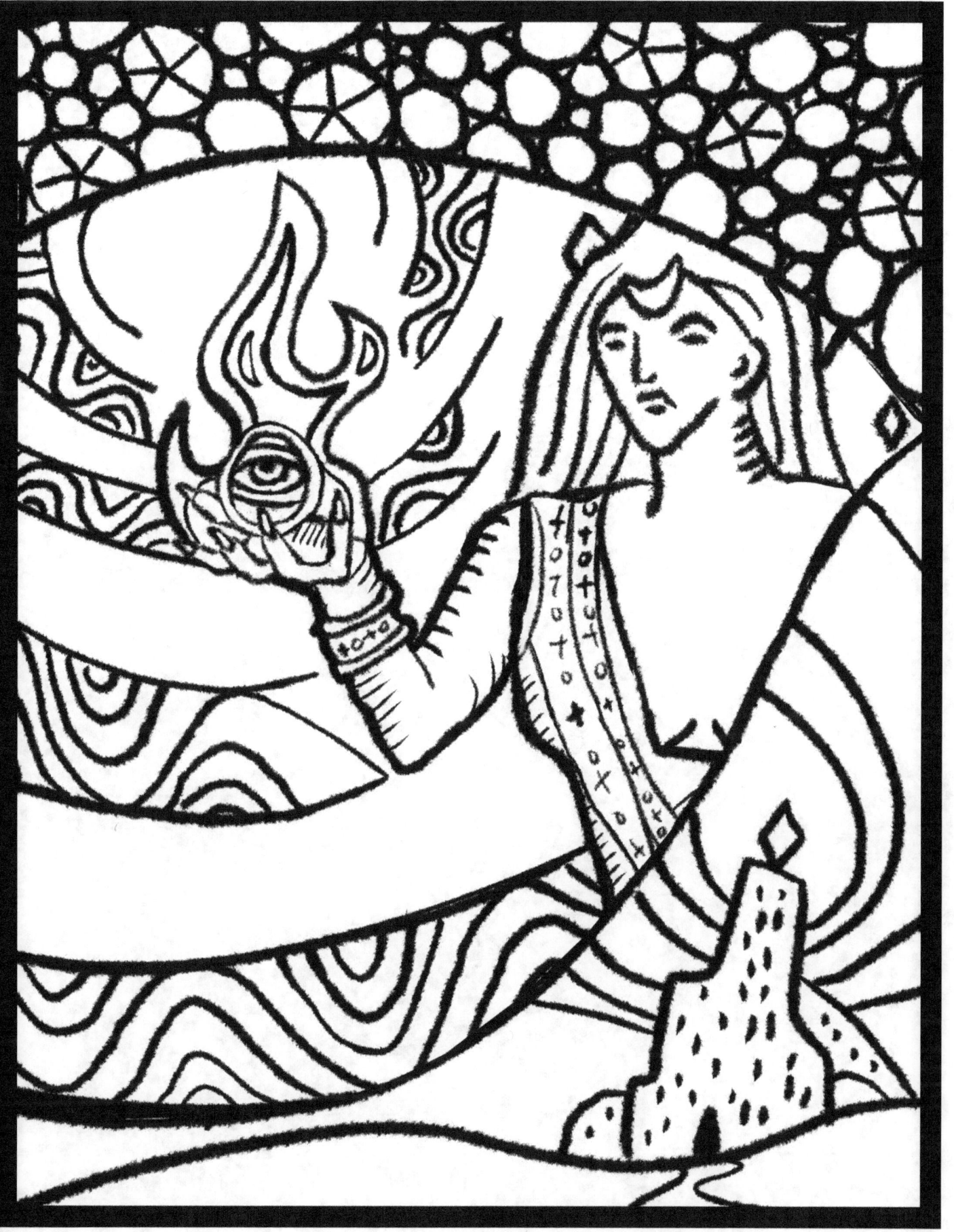

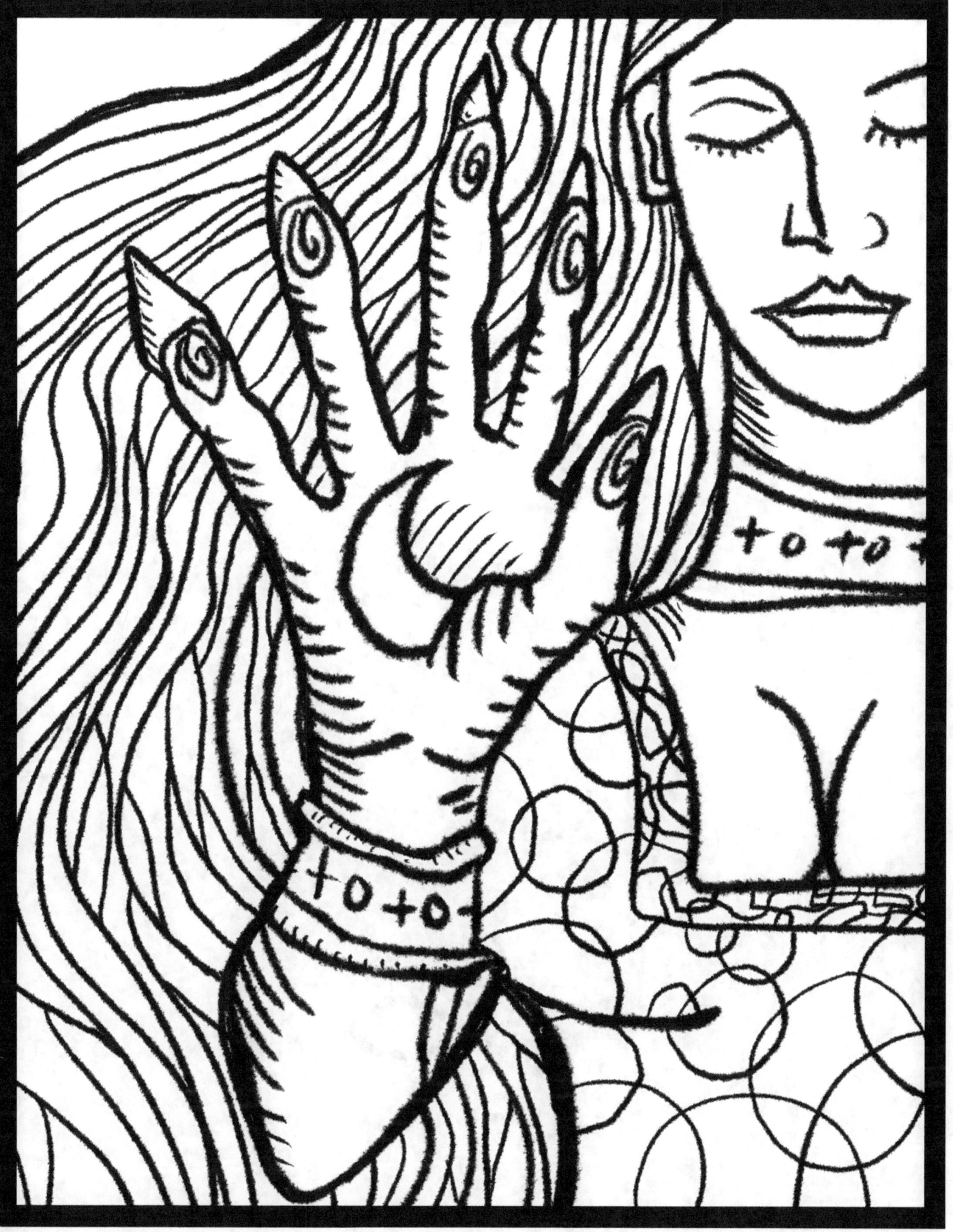

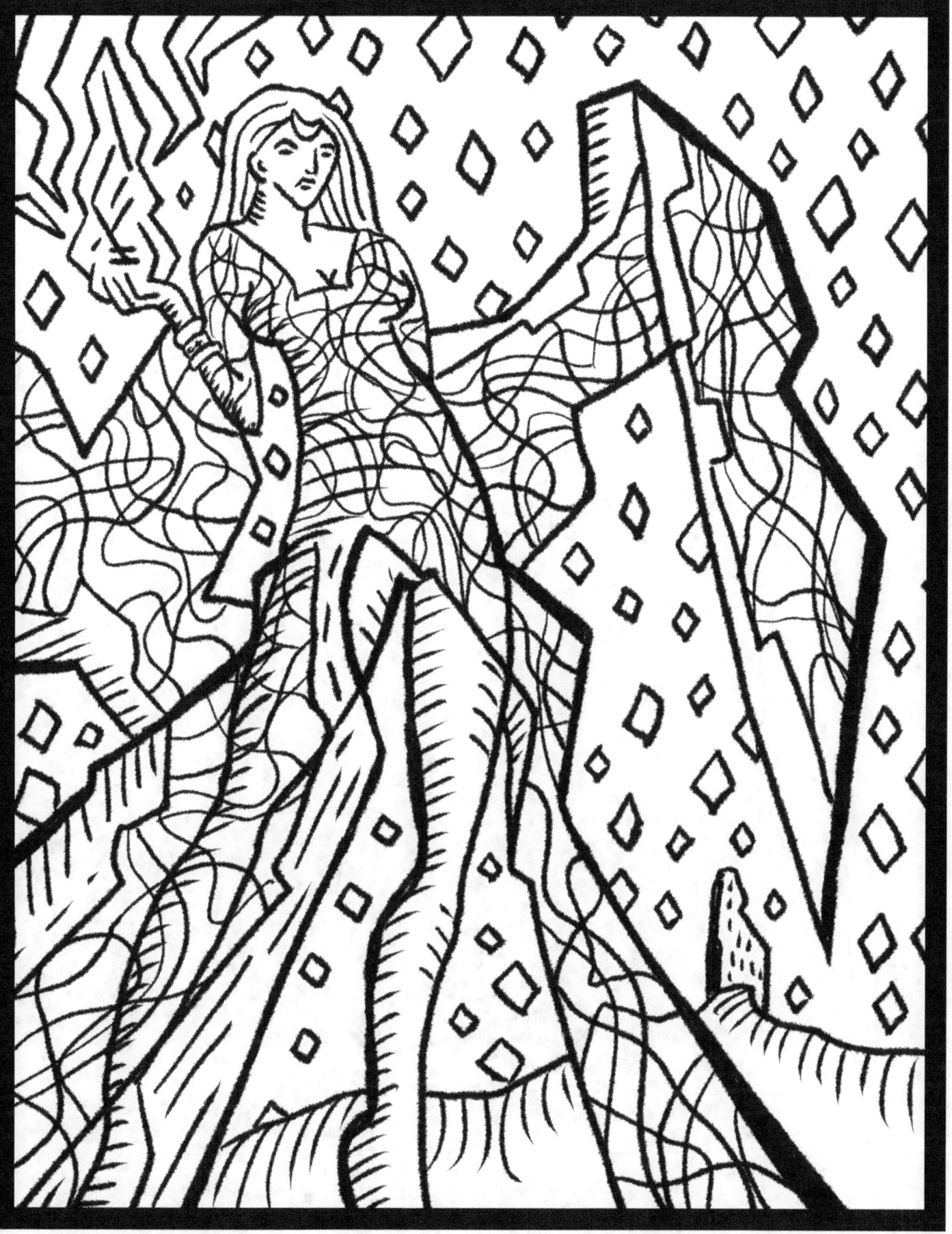

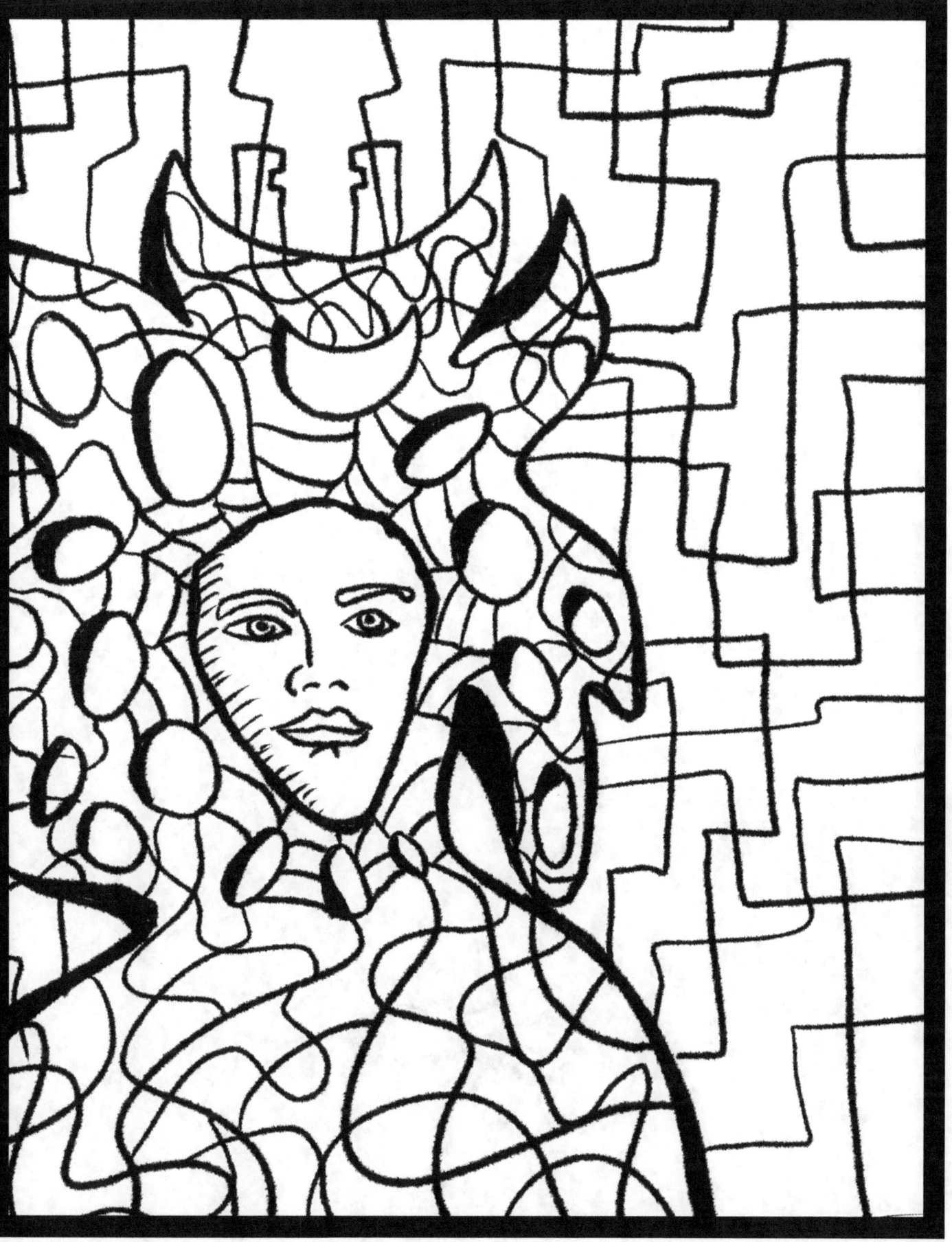

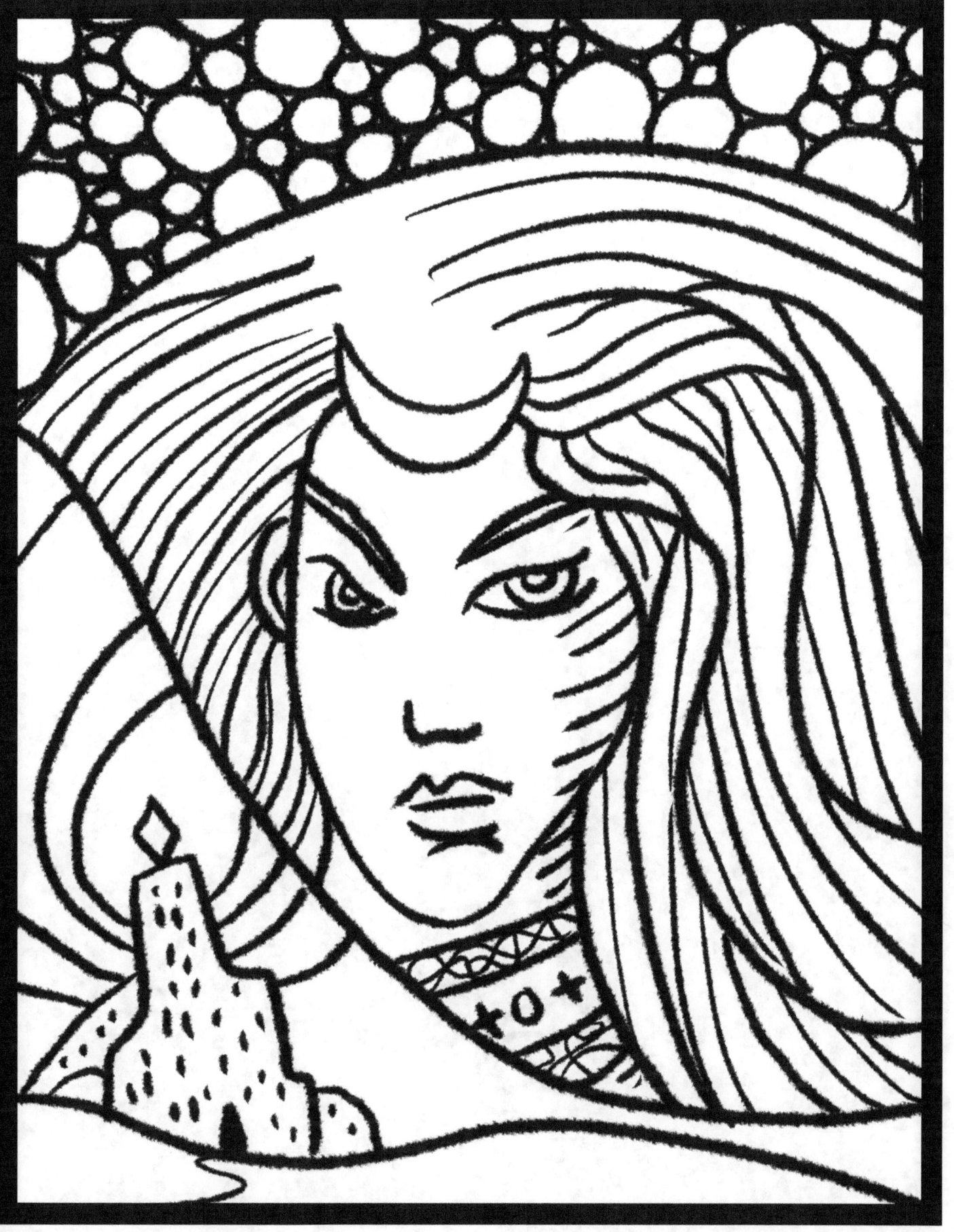

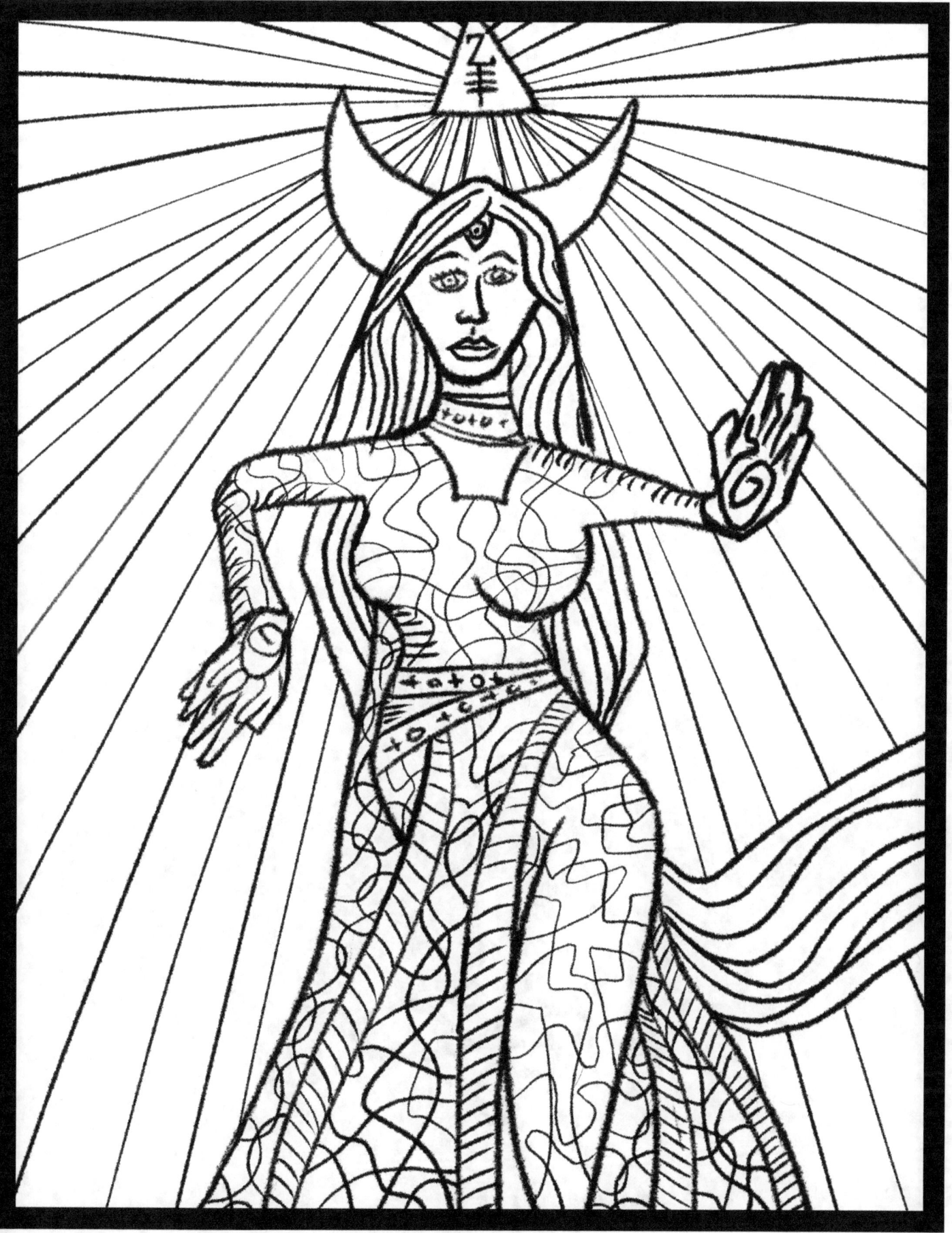

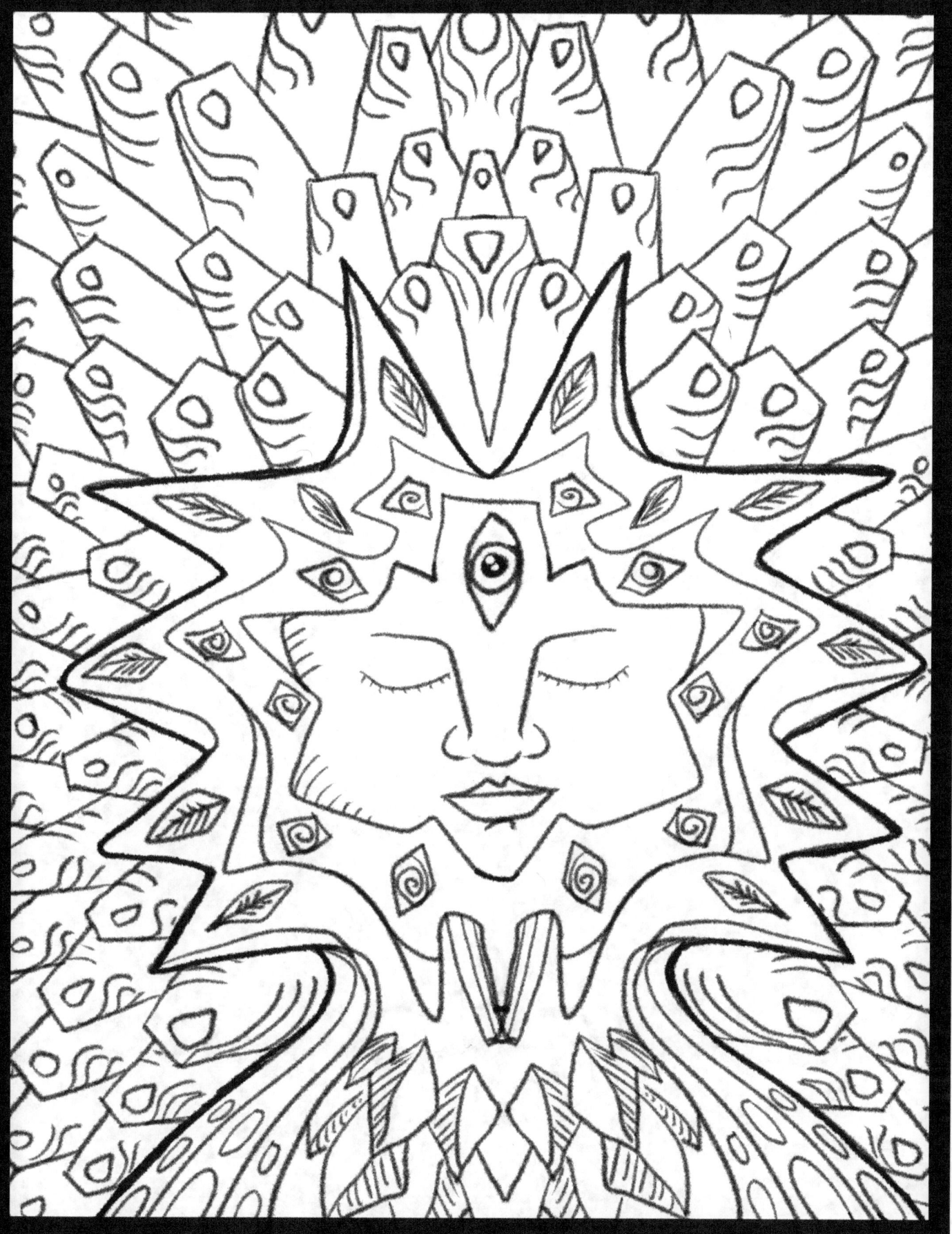

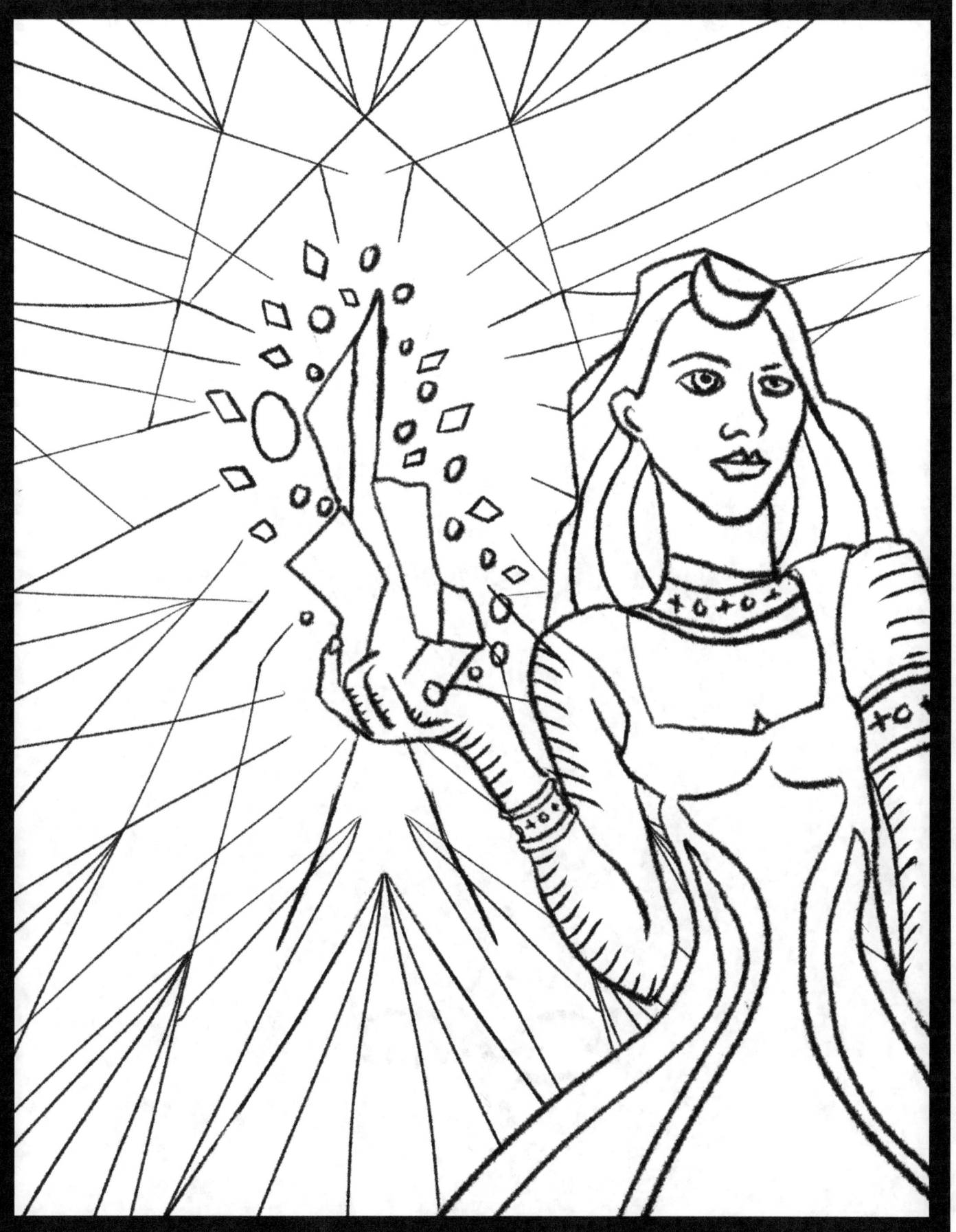

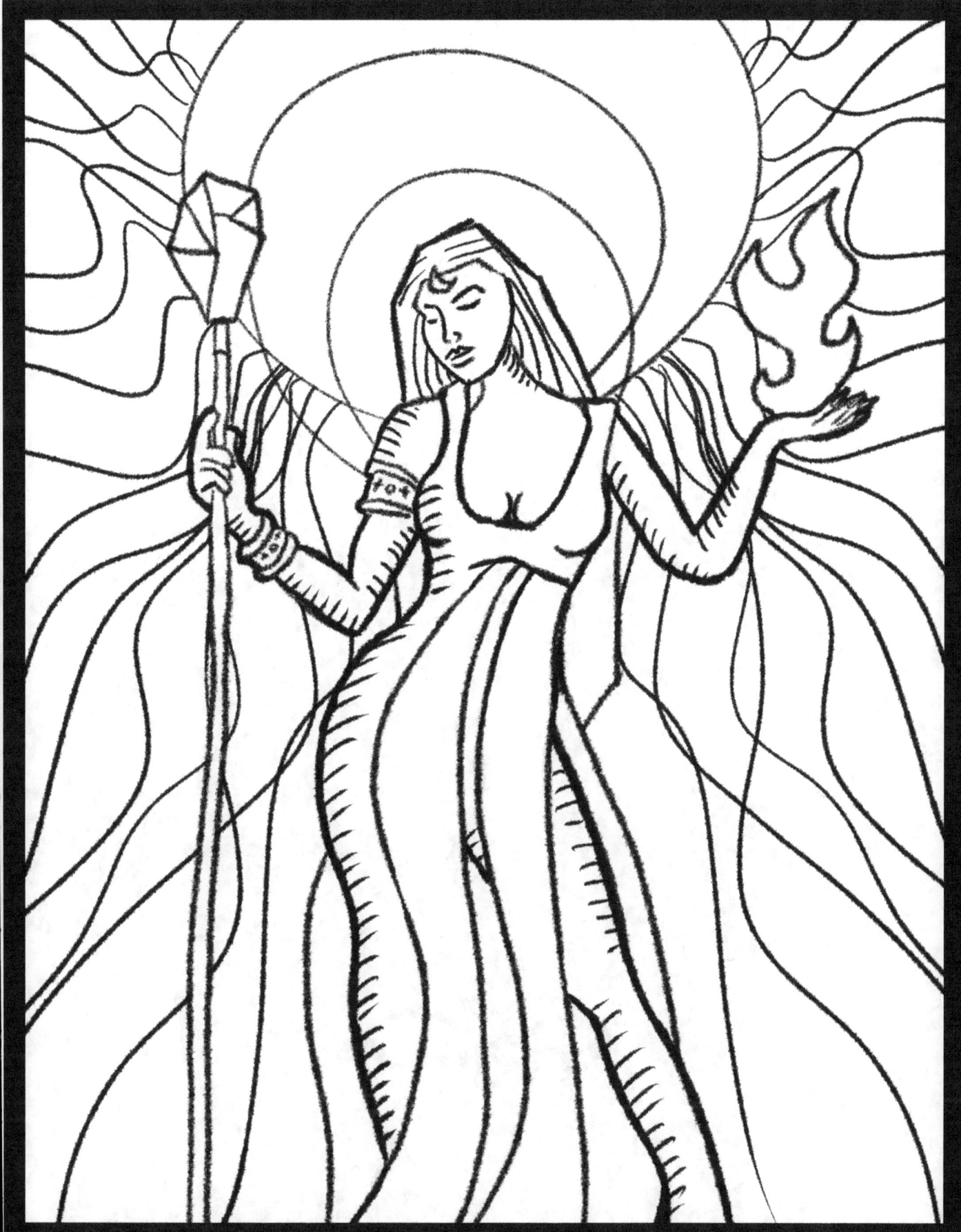

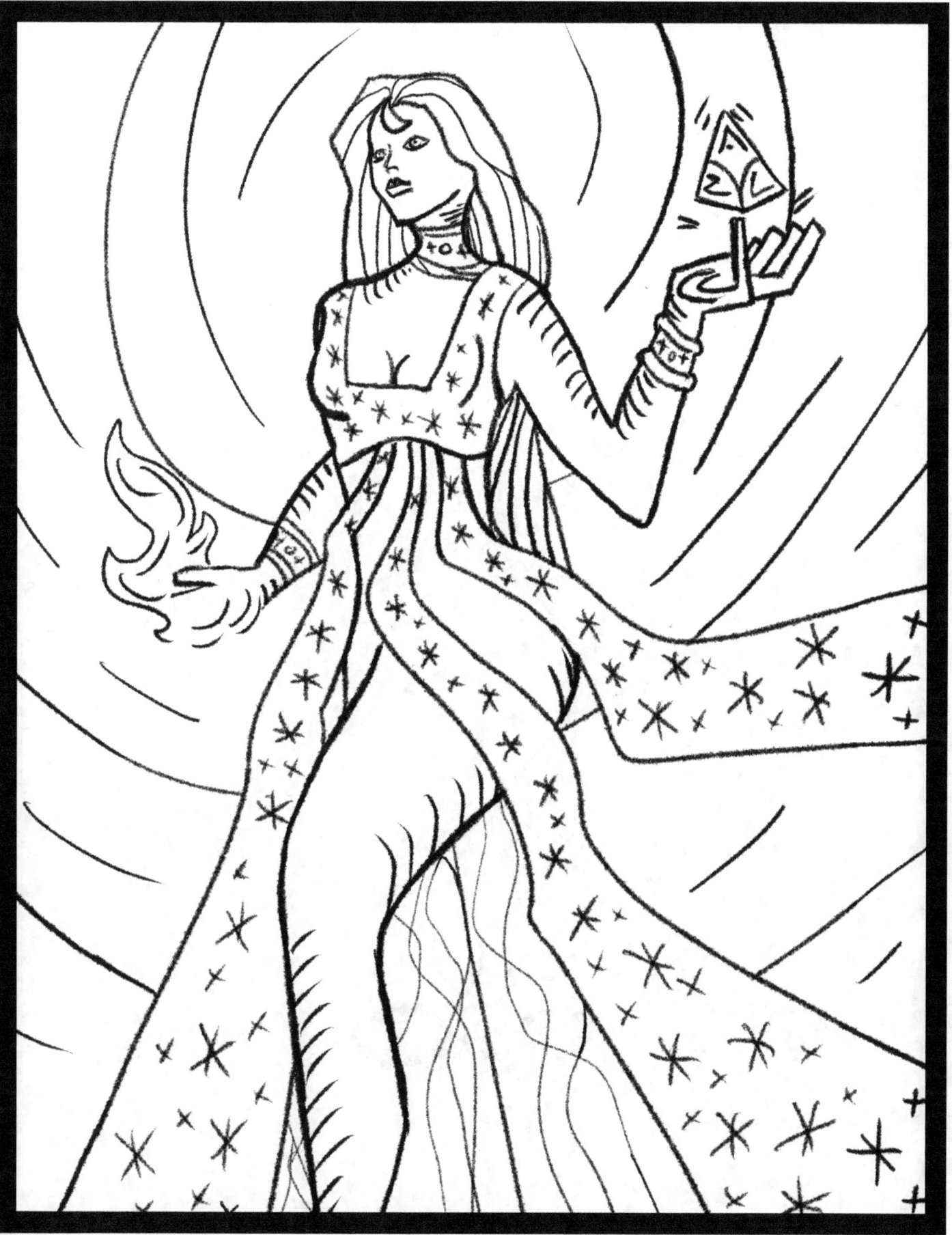

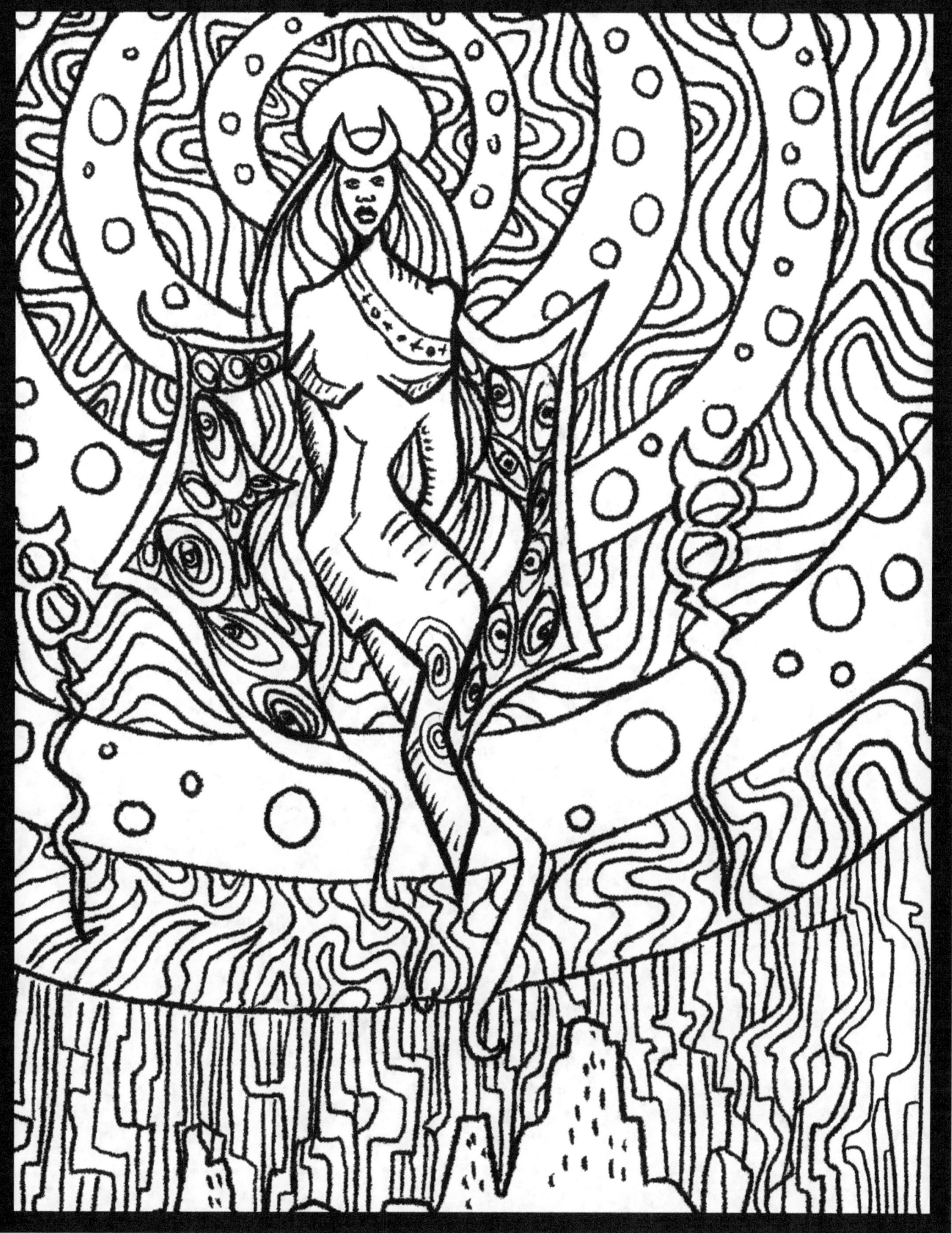

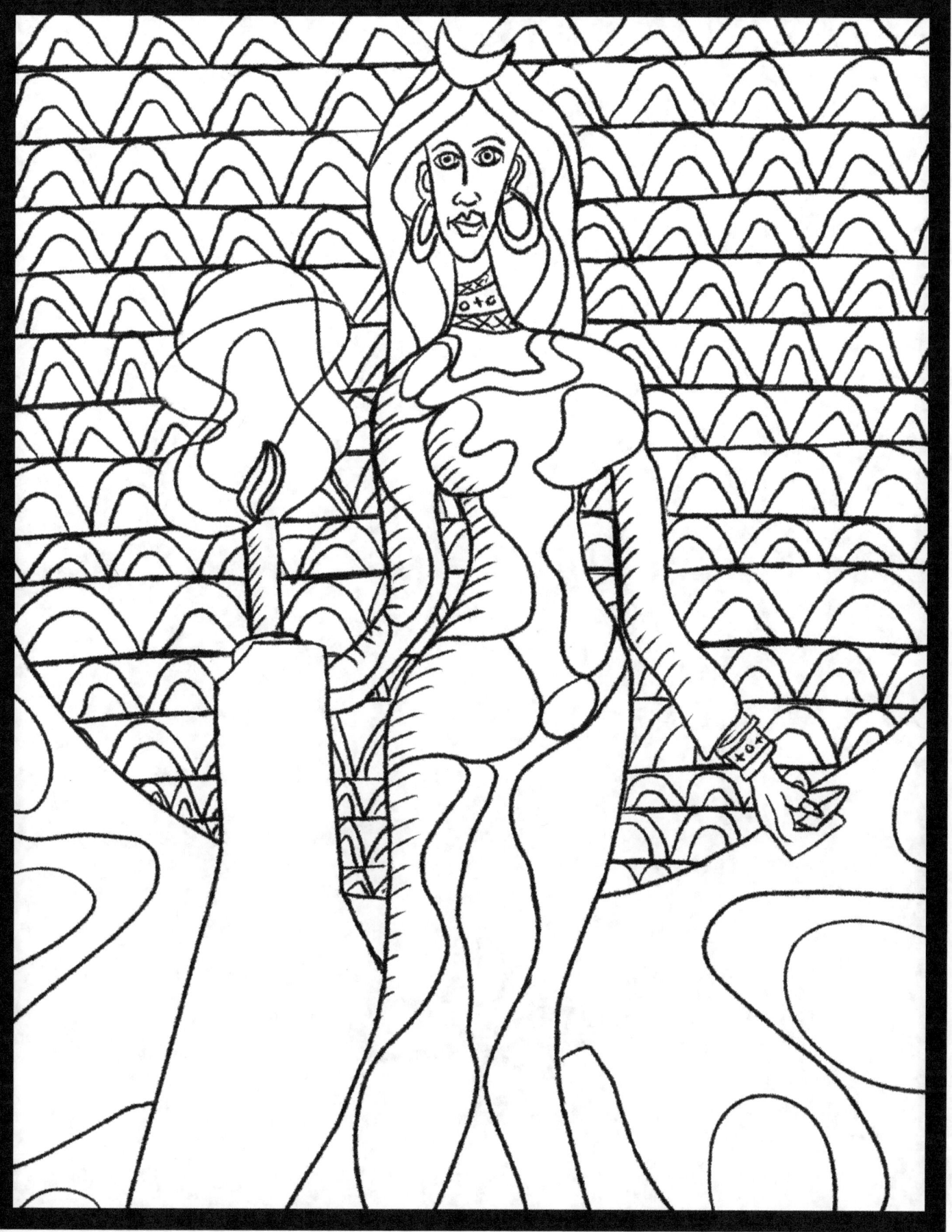

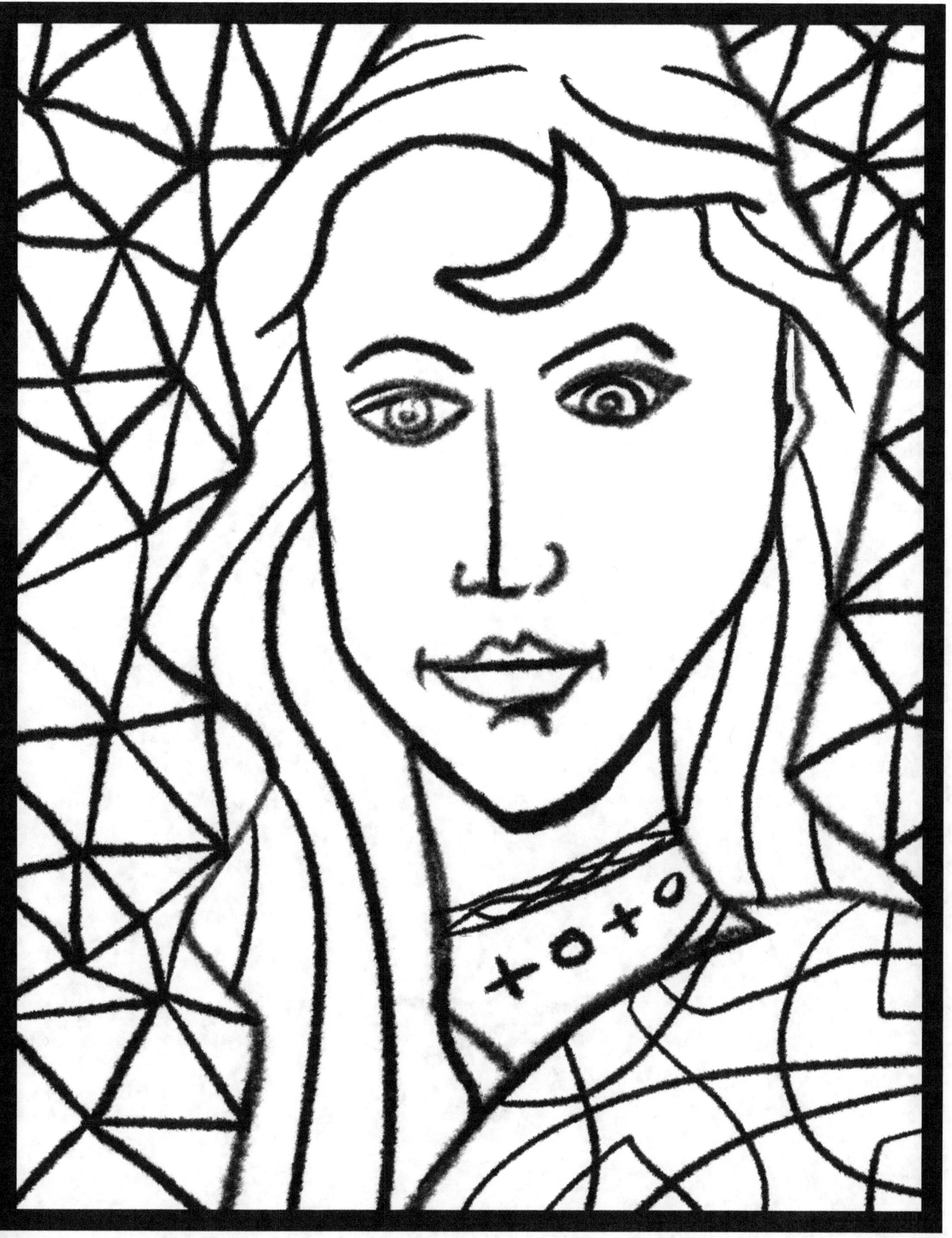